PTSD

Recover From Traumatic Stress in Adulthood

(Post Traumatic Stress Disorder Symptoms and Regaining Emotional Balance)

Henry Nelson

Published by Tomas Edwards

© **Henry Nelson**

All Rights Reserved

Ptsd: Recover From Traumatic Stress in Adulthood (Post Traumatic Stress Disorder Symptoms and Regaining Emotional Balance)

ISBN 978-1-990268-55-7

Legal & Disclaimer

The information contained in this book is not designed to replace or take the place of any form of medicine or professional medical advice. The information in this book has been provided for educational and entertainment purposes only.

The information contained in this book has been compiled from sources deemed reliable, and it is accurate to the best of the Author's knowledge; however, the Author cannot guarantee its accuracy and validity and cannot be held liable for any errors or omissions. Changes are periodically made to this book. You must consult your doctor or get professional medical advice before using any of the suggested remedies, techniques, or information in this book.

Upon using the information contained in this book, you agree to hold harmless the Author from and against any damages, costs, and expenses, including any legal fees potentially resulting from the application of any of the information provided by this guide. This disclaimer applies to any damages or injury caused by the use and application, whether directly or indirectly, of any advice or information presented, whether for breach of contract, tort, negligence, personal injury, criminal intent, or under any other cause of action.

You agree to accept all risks of using the information presented inside this book. You need to consult a professional medical practitioner in order to ensure you are both able and healthy enough to participate in this program.

Table of Contents

Introduction

Have you been to war? Or do you know a friend or a close family member who has been to war? Then this book is for you. This book guides both veterans and their loved ones through adjusting to life after warfare and overcoming the devastating symptoms of PTSD.

If you have a loved one who is a veteran of war, do you know what he or she has gone through and is still dealing with? Have you noticed significant differences from the person they were before they went to war and the person they have become after the war? Do you know that the events of the war could be haunting them in silence and could be the ones responsible for the sudden change in behavior, attitude and preferences? Well, your friend, father, mother, brother, son, daughter, sister or any other family member could be going through Post Traumatic Stress Disorder because of the war. They could be having flashbacks, nightmares, hallucinations and sleepless nights because of PTSD. They could also be having suicidal thoughts or thoughts of harming others.

Have you already started noticing some of those weird behavioral changes? Are you worried that your loved one might hurt him or herself or hurt someone else? Do you want to know how to help him or her adjust to life after warfare and even prevent any chances of the sudden changes affecting anyone in your family? This book will teach veterans and loved ones everything necessary to help your veteran overcome PTSD.

Thanks again for downloading this book, I hope you find it informative and useful!

Chapter 1: Understanding PTSD

Post-traumatic stress disorder (PTSD) is an anxiety disorder, a condition that results from a person experiencing stressful or traumatic events. The person has experienced events that he or she has difficulty coping with or adjusting to. These events and difficulties can then lead to symptoms that necessitate treatment.

Post-traumatic stress disorder develops in different ways for different people. At times, the symptoms may already be present a few hours after the traumatic event or sometimes it may take days or weeks before the symptoms will show.

What causes PTSD?

PTSD can come from different causes:

Family Violence – This has been a contributing factor to the occurrence of PTSD among children of school age. Studies reveal that the experiences of violence among children may contribute to the development of PTSD. The disorder does not develop directly after the traumatic event but it is the flashbacks and the nightmares that are the contributing factors to the development of the disorder. The experience of child abuse may interact with the stress-related gene mutation that increases the risk of PTSD in adulthood.

Genes – This is another cause of PTSD. A person's mental health inheritance may increase his risk of developing PTSD.

Life experiences – The traumatic experiences that a person has had actually increases the risk of PTSD development. However, this does not mean that all who have experienced traumatic events will develop the said disorder. Depending on the amount and the severity of the trauma, PTSD may occur.

Here are some of the life experiences that may lead to PTSD:

Rape

Assault

Vehicular accidents

Natural disasters

Acts of terrorism

War

Domestic abuse

A combination of these experiences and how the person reacts to these events will predispose one to develop PTSD.

What are the symptoms of PTSD?

Post-traumatic stress disorder has different symptoms in different people. Here are the symptoms that you may find in people with PTSD. The symptoms of the said disorder can be grouped into three categories:

Symptoms of re-experiencing – These are the symptoms wherein the person is constantly reminded of what has happened:

Flashbacks – This is when the person relives the traumatic event over and over again.

Bad dreams – Nightmares happen to the person to remind him of the traumatic event that he went through.

Frightening thoughts – This is when a sudden frightening thought comes to the person.

Symptoms of avoidance:

Avoiding talking about the event or even thinking about it

The feeling of being emotionally numb

Avoiding certain activities that the person usually does

Does not see any future

Inability to concentrate

Having problems with memory

Inability to have close relationships

Increased emotional arousal

Irritable or easily angered

Self-destructive activities like excessive unhealthy vices

Sleep problems

Hyper-vigilance

Being easily startled

A combination of these symptoms may be present in people with PTSD.

Children with PTSD, however, may have different symptoms compared to what adults may have experienced. In younger children, the symptoms may include bedwetting even if they already know how to use the toilet, the inability to talk or forgetting how to talk, acting out scary events during play time, and being very clingy to adults or people whom they are comfortable with. In teens, PTSD symptoms may include disrespectful or disruptive behaviors. They may also be self-destructive and may feel guilty for not preventing deaths. Some teens may have constant thoughts of revenge.

Understanding what PTSD is and how it occurs as well as its symptoms can help us detect the said disorder early on and thus enable us to address it immediately.

Chapter 2: Recognizing Symptoms of PTSD

Anyone who has experienced trauma will experience some level of stress. And since the line between acute stress disorder and PTSD are made up of the length of time and severity of effects, prevention is half the battle. You will want to take steps to mitigate any kind of stress that could turn into PTSD.

To do that, you need to keep an eye out for the red lights. For this, you'll need to know how to tell if a person is either at risk of or currently experiencing PTSD. When looking out for the disorder, doctors normally point out three things, namely:

☐The presence of identifiable triggers

☐The severity of the symptoms

☐The length of time that they have lasted

By using this holistic approach, it makes it easier for you to safely and correctly conclude that someone has PTSD.

What are the symptoms to watch out for?

Recurring, invasive thoughts:

Take note if the patient complains or talks about certain thoughts and notions that he or she cannot seem to shake off. If you chance upon someone who seems to always be in deep thought or bothered by something, try asking the person what's on his or her mind. If it happens to be the same concern over and over again, that person is experiencing recurring and invasive thoughts.

For example: if a person who once got involved in a car crash could be constantly worried that the vehicle he or she is riding isn't safe. The person may look behaved inside the car, but inside the mind is the constant need to get out of the car.

These thoughts are so strong that even if the patient is aware that the thoughts are mere imagination, they still feel very compelling, as if what they've experienced before is something that can happen to them again.

Indifference or avoidance:

People who experience PTSD are likely to lose a huge part of their lives because of the fear of reliving a past event. You know that feeling when something bad happens to you and you just don't want to talk about it? It's like that, only more intense. People who have PTSD will literally avoid everything that will make them think they might go through the same experience again.

For example: a person who witnesses a crime might not want to go to the witness stand because he or she will be forced to recount the witnessing. A person who almost drowned will avoid all kinds of water.

These people won't always behave wildly when they are exposed to these things. Sometimes, they will pretend that they can get by without them. This is particularly dangerous because the subject of the patient's fears could be something he or she could be helped with.

Panic attacks:

People with PTSD can be very paranoid. They jump at the sound of small pops or bangs or have recurring nightmares. Their hyper-sensitivity can also come in many different forms. These are people who will feel irritable a lot. Some of them can't get enough rest. They get upset about anything easily.

Aside from having a short temper (when they never used to), and chronic irritability, they actually feel these panic attacks physically, in the form of heart palpitations, severe exhaustion (despite not doing anything), and even trouble sleeping.

Chapter 3: Sorrow

Grief is the acute pain that accompanies loss. Simply because it is a reflection of what we love, it can feel all-encompassing. Sorrow is not limited to the loss of people, but when it follows the loss of a loved one, it might be intensified by emotions of guilt and confusion, especially if the relationship was a tough one.

The Process of Sorrow

Because grief obeys its own trajectory, there is no timetable for emotions of pain after loss; nor is it possible to stay away from suffering altogether. Truth be told, tries to suppress or deny grief are just as likely to lengthen the process, while also demanding added psychological effort.

Likewise, the misperception that "more" grief is better or that there is a proper way to grieve can make the process more difficult.

For some people, sorrow is a short-term phenomenon, also referred to as severe sorrow, though the pain may return all of a sudden at a later time. But other people may experience extended sorrow, also known as complex grief, enduring months or years. Without help and support, such grief can result in isolation and persistent isolation.

Supporting a Griever

Because sorrow is experienced in many ways, experts suggest that those who would support a good friend or loved one in a time of grieving follow that person's lead, and resist judging whether they appear to be insufficiently sad or to be dwelling in sorrow for too long. And it is typically unhelpful to encourage the pursuit of "closure."

Offering practical help and a recognition of a loss are both positive actions. Many mourners want those around them to listen, ask questions, and share memories, consequently verifying the depth and validity of the griever's emotions and helping them recover.

What We Mourn.

It is expected that somebody will grieve after the loss of a parent, brother or sister, partner, kid, or buddy. However, those are not the only losses that cause sorrow. Many people might grieve the loss of a treasured pet, a job or other crucial role in life, or a house or other mentally significant possessions. And it typically takes place after a divorce.

Sadly, many find that those around them do not acknowledge these forms of grief, which is exactly why they are identified disenfranchised: The strong pain is intensified by the internal feeling that one has not been given "consent" to experience it. However, the framework of grieving can help an individual work through such moment of chaos, particularly if those around them respond with compassion, and recognize that an individual is entitled to anger, numbness, and nonlinear healing.

Chapter 4: Dig the Defense: Holistic PTSD Treatments

"I went to a bookstore and asked the saleswoman, 'Where's the self-help section?' She said if she told me, it would defeat the purpose."
— George Carlin

Based on your holistic growth and engagement in mindful exercises and tips from Chapter 2 as far as recognizing some of the integrated effects of complex PTSD regarding physical, socioemotional, psychological, spiritual, behavioral, vocational, cognitive, sexual, financial, and other aspects, Chapter 3 will now include some holistic PTSD treatment ideas that can help you to deeply dig the defenses in your own life and healing journey.

If you are a sports fan or athlete, then you automatically understand how defensive strategies are essential for any teams' or participants' successes, right? Since this workbook is more practical, hands-on, and anecdotal, rather than clinical and solely theoretical, this chapter is merely an overview for what is currently out there, so you can choose to add to your own needs and preferences when coping with complex PTSD:

Story Glory: Consider cognitive therapy to work through trauma and complex PTSD. Experts explain how therapists guide patients "to recognize the traumas they've experienced as small parts of their life stories" ("Warning Signs and Ways to Help," 2001).

In particular, one article that I strongly endorse for you to read on your own is by Ramsey (2019) called "Make Anxiety Your Superpower" (https://www.scribd.com/article/4019373 81/Make-Anxiety-Your-Superpower). It comprehensively praises the power of CBT to reboot your mind and help us to "better understand, express, and reframe their internal emotional experience. CBT is based on the premise that much of our distress is caused by faulty thinking patterns. You learn to recognize cognitive distortions such as all-or-nothing thinking, catastrophizing, and scolding yourself" (https://www.scribd.com/article/4019373 81/Make-Anxiety-Your-Superpower).

Instead of being merely a character in your own horror or tragic stories, CBT allowed me to use journaling, photography, mindfulness, yoga, and other means to tell my story and rewrite new chapters in a positive, resilient manner. What can you do with CBT to set you free from complex PTSD? Allow CBT to be your candle and shine on!

Face Off: While this type has nothing to do with beauty, mirrors, or dermatology, exposure therapy might be an option for you since professionals literally expose clients to a situation that can cause trauma and panic. The sufferer addresses the triggers under a therapist's guidance.

There are even studies to support how virtual reality exposure therapies are gaining praise. Techies and gamers will love these suggestions!

When I engaged in this type of therapeutic work, I was finally able to glue all the pieces into where and why I was struggling. Exposure therapy is tough, but it makes you feel like a superhero after mastering it! Move over Avengers!

Mind over Matter: Yoga, meditation, and other forms of mindfulness healing in the here and now are extremely popular with patients suffering from PTSD. This book devotes all of Chapter 8 to this approach, so you can move from "a mind full of trauma" to a mindful mindset more autonomously.

Mindfulness meditation has literally saved my life. I am now so much more skilled at "chillaxing" and finding the peace within me to quiet my mind, body, and soul, keys to healing from complex PTSD. Are you ready to OM out with me today?

Tag Team: Group therapy is often a viable way to address complex PTSD in many cases due to the social support and ability to share experiences. When we are able to talk with and listen to others who have experienced similar events, we feel authentic support and immense validate. Check out what group therapy sessions are available in your city or town. There are also tons of online opportunities that you may enjoy, too.

Eye of the Tiger: Not, the iconic song or zoo animal, but studies reveal how eye-movement therapy is receiving kudos as a holistic helper since rapid eye movement may help the brain to process traumatic memories more naturally ("Warning Signs and Ways to Help, 2001, p 52). It is technically called Eye movement desensitization and reprocessing or EMDR and operates EMDR was developed as a treatment for traumatic memories as the client performs rhythmic eye movements while simultaneously concentrating on that painful recollection.

I worked with a therapist a few years ago in EMDR. It was really amazing how jittery and fight/flight my eyes were before starting the sessions. He helped me to relax and find ways to release the memories and move into the present and future with bliss, surrender, confidence, and empowerment.

DBT and Me: DBT is short for dialectical behavior therapy, an approach that develops emotion-regulation skills across a variety of mental disorders by using mindfulness and attentiveness to emotions, thoughts, and feelings, in conjunction with cognitive and behavioral treatments, according to Jubb (2017) in "The Effectiveness of Self-Soothing Techniques for People With PTSD in Secure Units" from Mental Health Practice.

As a verbal person, DBT was my cup of tea because I was able to verbally process and articulate many of the horrific events that I had suppressed and repressed.

Make It Rain With Reiki: Reiki applies the notion that we all have energy fields around our bodies that can be influenced by others. No umbrellas are required, though. Find a local professional who is experienced and certified in this time of trauma and energy work.

Tap Out Trauma: Tapping is not the cool dance genre in the context of therapeutic practices. Instead, it refers to a type of sensory stimulation that aims to rid the body, mind, and spirit of any negative energy (EFT and Tapping for Beginners: The Essential EFT Manual to Start Relieving Stress, Losing Weight, and Healing, 2013). Gaesser (2018) claims how it falls under the treatment called EFT, which stands for the Emotional Freedom Technique, an evidenced-based anxiety management intervention

(https://www.researchgate.net/publicatio
n/327846630_Befriending_Anxiety_to_Re
ach_Potential_Strategies_to_Empower_O
ur_Gifted_Youth).

Like reiki, it aims to activate energy points in the body, similar to acupuncture-- except without the needles" (EFT and Tapping for Beginners: The Essential EFT Manual to Start Relieving Stress, Losing Weight, and Healing, 2013). Check it out for yourself if the idea interests you to try and tap out the trauma in a holistic manner.

"Our past may explain why we're suffering but we must not use it as an excuse to stay in bondage." — Joyce Meyer, Battlefield of the Mind: Winning the Battle in Your Mind

Self-Care Flair: Consider massage and/or acupuncture for some back to the basic, self-care flair. As Meyer's quote reflects, we can stop the excuses and start taking care of ourselves to escape those shackles that may bind us to our pasts and pains. Create a game plan today to add more self-care flair into your life and daily regimens:

1.

_____

_____

2.

_____

_____

3.

_____

_____

My examples:

Journaling before bed

Bubble baths

Essential oils

Connect with Your Crew: Faith-based support is also helpful, so connect with community resources and mentors, if applicable. Gather a support system of trusted friends, loved ones, family, colleagues or neighbors. Connect with your crew! Who's part of your recovery crew. Name them now:

1.

_____

_____

2.

_____

_____

3.

_____

_____

Say Yes Reflection:

"Forgiving isn't something you do for someone else. It's something you do for yourself. It's saying, 'You're not important enough to have a stranglehold on me.' It's saying, 'You don't get to trap me in the past. I am worthy of a future."
— Jodi Picoult, The Storyteller

I developed this exercise to encourage us from staying rigidly trapped into "no" habits or mindsets. In conjunction with Picoult's amazing quote, I also see this technique as a door to forgiveness. In turn, literally "say yes" to each of the above treatment types and list at least 2-3 possible benefits of trying the approach. When we open ourselves with "yes" responses, we simultaneously open our minds, bodies, hearts, and spirits to healing and self-empowerment more readily from complex PTSD.

Example:

Yes, I will try cognitive therapy because I love to write and want to share my stories with other survivors.

Try your own **Say Yes** ideas here:

1.

_____

_____

2.

_____

_____

3.

_____

_____

4.

_____

_____

5.

_____

_____

Chapter 5: Etiology of PTSD

Etiology is the study of the causes or origins of PTSD. Aside from the obvious cause of a traumatic event, what makes one person more likely to develop PTSD than another who also suffered from the same trauma?

Many researchers believe that a neurobiological predisposition must exist for a person to develop PTSD. "Those likely to develop PTSD tend to have a pre-existing depression or anxiety disorder, or a family history of anxiety and neuroticism." xxii

As discussed in Chapter One under "Neurobiological Effects," the trauma's affect on the brain is what differentiates PTSD from a flight or fight response. "In a normal fear response, the immediate sympathetic discharge activates the "fight-or-flight" reaction. Increases in both catecholamines and cortisol occur relative to the severity of the stressor. Cortisol release stimulated by corticotropin-releasing factor via the hypothalamic-pituitary-adrenal (HPA) axis acts in a negative feedback loop to suppress sympathetic activation and cause further release of cortisol." xxiii

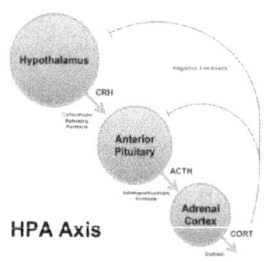

HPA Axis

In PTSD patients, cortisol levels are lower than normal, which is attributed to chronic "adrenal exhaustion." Recent research shows that patients involved in car accidents who had significantly lower than normal cortisol levels just after the accident were more likely to go on to develop PTSD. In a related study, women with a previous history of rape showed lower levels of cortisol after a rape than other victims of similar attacks. This has led researchers to a hypothesis that "the HPA axis and the sympathetic nervous system are disassociated in persons who develop PTSD, which may allow for an uncontrolled catecholamine release that affects formation of memories during the trauma and perhaps exacerbates symptoms when that person is exposed to cues after the trauma." xxv

Traditional Treatment

Treatment of PTSD is highly individualized, depending on the patient's specific symptoms, trauma, co-disorders, and other needs. Generally speaking, "Treatment options include patient education, social support, and anxiety management through psychotherapy and psychopharmacologic intervention. Patient education and social support are important initial interventions to engage the patient and mitigate the impact of the traumatic event. Local and national support groups may help to de- stigmatize the mental health diagnosis and reaffirm that symptoms of PTSD involve more than just a reaction to stress and require treatment. Support from family and friends encourages understanding and acceptance that may alleviate survivor guilt. However, the mainstay of treatment is psychopharmacologic and psychotherapeutic intervention." xxvi

Psychotherapy

Psychotherapy, or counseling, involves meeting with a trained therapist on a regular basis. There are different types of psychotherapy that might be appropriate for someone suffering from PTSD. One study showed that 32 to 53 percent of PTSD patients who got 10 sessions of cognitive-behavioral treatment over a 16-week period showed a 50 percent reduction in the severity of their PTSD symptoms. xxvii Different types of counseling available for PTSD sufferers include:

"**Cognitive behavioral therapy** (CBT) is the most effective treatment for PTSD. There are different types of CBT such as cognitive therapy and exposure therapy.

1. One type is **Cognitive Processing Therapy** (CPT) where you learn skills to understand how trauma changed your thoughts and feelings.

2. Another type is **Prolonged Exposure** (PE) therapy where you talk about your trauma repeatedly until memories are no longer upsetting. You also go to places that are safe, but that you have been staying away from because they are related to the trauma.

A similar kind of therapy is called eye movement desensitization and reprocessing (EMDR). This therapy involves focusing on sounds or hand movements while you talk about the trauma." xxviii

Group therapy: "Joining a group of people who have been through similar

33

experiences can uplift and support an individual who is feeling alone and isolated with upsetting and traumatic memories and symptoms. Groups can lessen shame and provide community support as well as reduce feelings of helplessness. Groups for survivors of combat and sexual assault frequently involve members living with PTSD and related symptoms. The ancient expression "pain shared is pain halved" speaks to the relief people often feel when they share their stories with others." xxix

Exposure Therapy: "This behavioral therapy technique helps you safely face the very thing that you find frightening, so that you can learn to cope with it effectively. A new approach to exposure therapy uses "virtual reality" programs that allow you to re-enter the setting in which you experienced trauma — for example, a "Virtual Iraq" program."xxx

Exposure therapy, group therapy, and eye movement desensitization are less-used than cognitive-behavior treatment because their efficacy has not been thoroughly studied and demonstrated. About 14 percent of PTSD patients who are undergoing psychotherapy will drop out, with exposure therapy having the highest drop out rate (up to 50 percent).

Psychotherapy (especially group or family therapy) may also be useful for friends and family of the patient, due to the disruptive nature of having a friend or family member with PTSD. xxxi

Service Dogs

"The use of service dogs as forms of therapy for individuals living with PTSD, especially for veterans, is becoming increasingly common. A service dog is by a veteran's side 24 hours a day to help navigate daily stressors. Some animals come to the veteran pre-trained with a set of commands, while others are trained by the owners themselves. Over time, an owner can rely upon the dog's instincts for a reality check, giving their brain a break from hyper-vigilance. The animals can also serve as a social buffer, an incentive to exercise and a de-escalation tool during times of stress. See the resources section for more information on service dogs." xxxii

Pharmacology

There is no one specific medication given to help treat PTSD. Like psychotherapy, the selection of the appropriate medication is a highly individualized subject. Some types of medications that can be helpful include:

"**Antipsychotics**. In some cases, you may be prescribed a short course of

antipsychotics to relieve severe anxiety and related problems, such as difficulty sleeping or emotional outbursts.

Antidepressants. These medications can help symptoms of both depression and anxiety. They can also help improve sleep problems and improve your concentration. The selective serotonin reuptake inhibitor (SSRI) medications sertraline (Zoloft) and paroxetine (Paxil) are FDA-approved for the treatment of PTSD.

Anti-anxiety medications. These drugs also can improve feelings of anxiety and stress.

Prazosin. If your symptoms include insomnia or recurrent nightmares, a drug called prazosin (Minipress) may help. Prazosin, which has been used for years in the treatment of hypertension, also blocks the brain's response to an adrenaline-like brain chemical called norepinephrine.

Although this drug is not specifically approved for the treatment of PTSD, prazosin may reduce or suppress nightmares in many people with PTSD."xxxiv

Beta Blockers **xxxv**

Currently, only paroxetine (Paxil) and sertraline (Zoloft) are FDA approved for the treatment of PTSD. "In two separate 12-week, double-blind, placebo-controlled trials, both paroxetine and sertraline were found to be effective in the acute treatment of symptoms of PTSD. Of the patients who received 20 mg or 40 mg of paroxetine, 62 percent and 54 percent, respectively, responded positively compared with 37 percent of patients who received placebo. Patients who received a mean daily dosage of 146 mg of sertraline had a 60 percent positive response rate compared with a 38 percent positive response rate in patients receiving placebo."xxxvi

About 10 percent of PTSD patients are treated with antipsychotics- these are usually patients whose symptoms are most severe and intrusive. Clozapine, olanzapine, and risperidone have been shown to help reduce flashbacks, nightmares, and other PTSD symptoms.xxxvii

With antidepressants, patients can show reduced aggression, impulsivity, and suicidal thoughts. These medications can take up to eight weeks to work, and one class might not be as effective as another, so there is a level of trial and error associated with their use. A PTSD relapse is less likely if the patient has been on their medication for at least a year. Xxxviii

"Other less directly effective but nevertheless potentially helpful medications for managing PTSD include mood stabilizers like lamotrigine (Lamictal), tiagabine (Gabitril), and divalproex sodium (Depakote). Medicines that help decrease the physical symptoms associated with PTSD include drugs such as clonidine (Catapres), guaneficine (Tenex), and propranolol." xxxix

Chapter 6: Conditions Associated with PTSD

Post-traumatic Stress disorder and all other mental illnesses for the matter come with associated conditions that have a higher possibility of occurrence with the prevalence of an existing condition such as PTSD. These conditions could become more intense and worsen over time if left untreated and it is important to watch out for these signs in a person with PTSD in order for them to be treated thusly.

Alcohol or Substance Abuse:

This is the most commonly associated problem that often accompanies PTSD. Most PTSD sufferers and usually war veterans see alcohol and drugs as a way to calm themselves down and make themselves forget the traumatic events. This is due to the overwhelming experience that the PTSD has brought on their lives that even through the short effects of alcohol or substance abuse they are given relief if only for a moment, they find it worth it.

As this is the most common problem to be experienced by PTSD sufferers, then is it also the most difficult to deal with for those who offer support such as friends and family. The most common situation that occurs is that a relative tells a person that **'this is not that way to cope'** which will then be responded with **'you do not understand'** which puts the supporter at a dead end as often times, stating that you do understand could lead to anger.

When dealing with someone with PTSD who is showing signs of alcohol and substance abuse it is important to gradually put yourself in the middle of that behavior instead of just jumping in and saying STOP. Report this to the therapist if he is receiving counseling or seek help from other members of the family or from close friends to convince the sufferer to find treatment as with the presence of this additional condition, more harm is imminent.

Behavioral Changes Associated with Alcohol or Substance Abuse:

A person can become obviously more irritable and aggressive towards situations.

Simple obligations such as spending time with the family or going into work becomes hindered.

Taking alcohol or drugs even in situations when they know they shouldn't such as right before a big meeting or right before working manually in situations where heavy machinery or dangerous equipment is involved; or driving.

Legal problems begin to surface such as DUI's or minor aggression notices.

Quality of work produced no longer meets expectations.

Depression:

Depression is another common condition associated with the prevalence of Post-traumatic Stress Disorder. This could stem from a whole number of reason such as feeling pity or sadness for the people harmed in the traumatic event witnessed, feeling a deep sense of self-pity, or even feeling by knowing that there are people in the world who would do such things.

Dealing with depression is usually through therapy or medication but a strong support system can also greatly aid in the stabilization of a person and keep him from further declining or delving into depression. As a supporter, you should let the sufferer know that though there are such people and situations that would warrant as traumatic and bad, they are not here at present. Most importantly, remind the sufferer that they are in a safe environment and amongst good people.

Symptoms of Depression:

A deep sense of sadness and loss of hope.

Being unable to enjoy things that were once enjoyed. Losing interest and not caring.

Situations that could result in Depression besides PTSD:

Being in the military and having battle field experience.

Witnessing or being involved in violent attacks, crimes, sexual abuse, or child abuse.

Life-threatening Accidents

Natural calamities such as earthquakes, floods, tornadoes.

Suicide:

The next associated condition to PTSD is suicide which can stem from the previously mentioned depression if left untreated for a certain period of time. Suicide becomes a higher risk if treatment is not sought out or opted for and with a weak support system. It is important to realize that with the absence of treatment, for whatever reason, the support system must become even stronger.

What can increase suicide risk?

No support – not having anyone to talk to or empathize with can lead to a sufferer thinking increasingly about their traumatic situation with no one to stop them.

Having a family history of suicide – suicide specifically is not genetic, but mental illness is and all mental illnesses have the potential to lead to this.

Owning harmful equipment – your risk for suicide is greatly increased if you have a gun or knife collection. Or any other paraphernalia that could possibly make your decision easier.

Being male – it has been said that men are more likely to commit suicide then women. This is because men are less likely to divulge their feelings when they feel emotionally strained as compared to women.

Suicide warning signs:

Making plans to hurt yourself. Seeing a person take more interest in guns and such harmful equipment.

Thinking about suicide, imagining it happen. Hearing a sufferer talk increasingly about taking his life, even if it sounds like a joke.

When the sufferer owns an existing weapon or is seeking one out.

Having the feeling of being taken over and hearing voices whisper to your thoughts.

When a sufferer distances himself from everyone around him.

When a sufferer gives you one of his personal possessions that you know means a lot to him.

Anger:

Anger is a normal part of that stages to recovery but often times when faced by a traumatic event, especially one which has resulted in PTSD, a person is also then faced with the decision to 'fight or flight' and anger can be a condition experienced in accompaniment with PTSD if a person finds himself stuck in the 'fight' phase where they stay paranoid and constantly on alert for similar situations.

Signs of Anger:

Being constantly on alert for situations wherein harm might be caused to you or to others.

Being convinced that violence and negative reinforcement is the answer to all problems.

Feeling paranoid and afraid of things that don't really pose a threat.

Dealing with Anger:

If you are already seeing a therapist, tell him about your increased irritability and agitation and suggest further anger management besides your PTSD treatment sessions.

If you are feeling a surge of range coming along or you have been angered by a previous occurrence and are now transferring to a different scene, step out for a bit and get a breather until you calm down.

Practice empathy. If anyone has said something that angers you, try to view their reasons. They might be harmless and not said to directly anger you in the first place.

Express your feelings by any means you want. Either by talking to someone, keeping a journal, exercise, do artwork, music etc.

Avoid situations that make you angry in every way. This can be done physically, and visually as well by avoiding movies that you know are bad for your mental state.

Try doing relaxation techniques such as deep breathing exercises, meditation, exercises, or yoga.

Grief:

Grief is another symptom on the road to complete treatment. This is characterized by feeling sad for yourself or for other people by being in a certain situation. Grief can also be the cause for PTSD by the sudden and unexpected loss of someone very close to you such as a loved one, a long time pet, or a valuable keepsake.

Causes of Grief:

Sudden death of someone very close to you.

The end of an important relationship such as going through a break-up with someone who has been in a relationship with you for a long time, or divorce.

Losing your job

Retirement – as this could mean the loss of daily routine and changes to what you are used to.

Death of a pet

Moving away

Being a witness to or present for any untoward situations such as robberies, attacks, or natural calamities.

The grieving process:

There is no standard way to grieve, as different as people are from one another, so is the difference of the grieving process and how they prefer to do things. Below are some samples of experiencing grief.

Feeling fatigues even without any physical stimuli. Experiencing dyspnea or shortness of breath, trouble sleeping or restlessness.

Feeling emotionally suppressed by fear, anxiety, or anger.

Being socially incapable of normal reactions. Overreacting, and avoiding other people such as friends, family, and work colleagues.

Wondering why this happened to you out of all the people it could possibly happen to.

Dealing with Grief:

Taking care of yourself by eating right and sleeping enough.

Allow others to support you by letting them in.

Exercise for a healthier body and also to keep your mind off of things.

Consider joining a support group.

Have a go-to person who you feel comfortable talking to and who listens.

Remember what or who you are grieving.

Let your feelings out. Do not bottle them up.

Panic Attacks:

Closely associated with anxiety disorder and mental illness, panic attacks are experienced in the midst of a Post-Traumatic Stress Disorder breakdown in the presence of a trauma trigger. When a person experiences the trauma again and relives it through thoughts or dreams, panic is inevitable.

Signs of a Panic Attack:

Chest tightness and pain

Tachycardia or a fast heartbeat.

Dizziness and tremors in extremities

Nausea

Breaking out in a sweat

Hot flashes or chills

A choking feeling

Having to deal with all these associated conditions can be easily avoided with therapy and counseling early into the PTSD and as soon as it is realized or diagnosed.

When dealing with a loved one who has PTSD, it is important to simply be there. If they are easily irritated or agitated, the best thing you can do sometimes is simply to offer your presence even if it means not doing or saying anything. People with PTSD have already been though a lot and might still be going through them on occasion, and with the presence of any one of these associated conditions, their situation will only become worse and substantially more difficult to deal with; do not add to the stress by forcing a treatment method or medication, instead try your best to understand in order to first bring the sufferer to a calm state.

Chapter 7: What is Post-Traumatic Stress Disorder (PTSD)?

We all experience terrible and frightening events at certain points in our lives. And along with these experiences, it is only normal for us to feel afraid, nervous, and anxious, to have a hard time forgetting what happened, or to be able to sleep well after the incident.

These feelings and experiences are considered to be normal reactions of the body to such situations and typically, these unpleasant emotions eventually ebb over time and the individual involved is able to successfully get back to his or her normal day to day life. However, this is not always the case for everyone.

For some people, the unpleasant emotions that come with a terrifying experience become seemingly insurmountable, even long after the horrifying event has already passed. The feelings of fear and being in constant danger do not fade over time and could even become worse and serious enough to cause severe disruptions in the different aspects of the life of the individual. This is what constantly haunts individuals who suffer from a certain condition known as **Post-Traumatic Stress Disorder (PTSD)**.

Understanding the Basics of PTSD

Post-Traumatic Stress Disorder, or simply **PTSD**, is a serious mental health condition which could primarily develop after an individual has experienced or witnessed a particular traumatic event wherein severe physical harm has been inflicted or the overall safety and wellbeing of the person has been gravely threatened.

Examples of events or incidents which could seriously inflict trauma and could have the possibility of leading to PTSD are:

Serious accidents

Physical or sexual abuse

Torture

Violence or war

Natural disasters

Assault

Sudden or terrifying death of a loved one

Kidnapping

Abuse and neglect during childhood

PTSD is primarily characterized by severe anxiety, flashbacks, as well as uncontrollable fearful thoughts long after the occurrence of the traumatic event and even when there is already no more threat of any danger. These symptoms may become severe enough such that the normal course of the life of the individual is profoundly disrupted.

This certain condition could affect not just the individual who experience the terrifying event firsthand but also others who witness the occurrence and even those who pick up the pieces subsequently, such as emergency responders, law enforcement officers, paramedics, and family members or loved ones of the person who personally experienced the trauma.

PTSD tends to develop in different ways among different individuals. While some of the symptoms of Post-Traumatic Stress Disorder may develop within hours or days after the terrifying experience, it may also take several weeks, months, or even years before they manifest themselves.

Normal Response to Trauma and PTSD: THE CORE DIFFERENCE

It is considered to be entirely normal to feel various kinds of strong emotions and physical reactions once a particular terrifying event has occurred. When in danger, it is only natural to feel anxious and fearful. In fact, this fear helps trigger the 'fight or flight' response of the body, a certain healthy reaction that triggers split-second changes in the body which in turn, prepares us to either defend ourselves and fight against the danger faced or to avoid and steer clear of it.

This certain reaction is triggered in the face of any immediate danger and is particularly meant to protect an individual from harm. However, for individuals suffering from PTSD, this reaction, which is originally meant to protect, becomes altered and instead, becomes detrimental to the individual. People who have Post-Traumatic Stress Disorder become extremely fearful even when the danger is already long gone.

When an individual's sense of safety and security is threatened or broken as a result of an unusually stressful circumstance, it is very common to experience the following normal responses to trauma:

PHYSICAL RESPONSES

Rapid breathing and palpitation

Trembling and cold sweats

Tightening of the stomach

Dizziness, fatigue, aches and pains, and muscle tension

Tight feeling in the throat

EMOTIONAL AND PSYCHOLOGICAL RESPONSES

Fear and anxiety

Being edgy, jumpy and having trouble concentrating

Vulnerability or helplessness

Shock and disbelief

Grief and sadness

Anger and resentment

Feeling numb and disconnected from others

Guilt and shame

For a lot of individuals who went through traumatic experiences, these feelings and reactions may make it difficult to cope and adjust and get back to their normal lives for a while, but they are not necessarily automatically diagnosed with Post-Traumatic Stress Disorder. Over time and with certain coping strategies, they are usually able to bounce back from the disaster, no matter how difficult the process can become.

However, for people with PTSD, these terrible feelings do not go away or even lessen after a long while and may even in fact, tend to get worse. Instead of being able to move on from the tragedy or incident, they become trapped in a state of psychological shock and this considerably prevents the person from living a normal and productive life.

Post-Traumatic Stress Disorder is a very difficult condition to deal with. It is like bringing your nightmares with you even during your waking hours. It is being stuck in the past and being uncontrollably haunted by memories that you would very much like to forget. It is like trying so hard to row the boat forward but having the tides strongly pull you back in and drown you in a whirlpool of intense fear and dread.

If left unattended, this serious condition could cause a considerable decline on the overall quality of life of the individual and may even inflict even greater damage to his or her overall safety and wellbeing.

Thus, if you or someone you care about suffers from this particular disorder, do not hesitate to ask for help and support or to offer some. Because while it is true that Post-Traumatic Stress Disorder is very difficult to face and deal with, it is also very important to be mindful of the fact that overcoming this particular disorder is also very much possible. It is something that you CAN, SHOULD, and WILL beat.

Signs and Symptoms of Post-Traumatic Stress Disorder (PTSD)

Post-Traumatic Stress Disorder (PTSD) may manifest itself differently from one person to another. The signs and symptoms of this particular mental health condition could occur either in a sudden or gradual manner and may come and go after a while. Sometimes, the symptoms may be triggered by someone or something that reminds the individual of the terrible incident while some other times, they may tend to just burst and arise out of the blue.

Despite certain differences in their manifestations from person to person, the various PTSD symptoms can be grouped into three major categories. These categories are:

Re-experiencing or reliving the traumatic event

Individuals who suffer from Post-Traumatic Stress Disorder may tend to go through re-experiencing symptoms which particularly involve reliving the traumatic event over and over again.

These symptoms could either start from the person's very own emotions and thoughts or could be triggered by certain objects, places, sensations, or situations that could considerably remind them of the traumatic event which occurred in the past.

Re-experiencing symptoms typically include:

Vivid flashbacks - feeling like the traumatic event is happening all over again

Intrusive and upsetting thoughts, memories, and images of the event

Nightmares or bad dreams about the incident or of other fearsome things o

events

Feelings of intense distress at actual or symbolic reminders of the traumatic event

Severe physical sensations or reactions when reminded of the trauma, such as rapid breathing, sweating, nausea, pounding heart, trembling and muscle tension

Avoidance and numbing

Another common symptom of individuals suffering from PTSD is trying to avoid things that could serve as reminders of the traumatic event and feeling emotionally numb. This set of symptoms may cause an individual to unusually change his or her personal routine as well as to lose interest in certain activities or in life as a whole.

Some avoidance and numbing symptoms include:

Repressing memories and as such, not being able to remember certain aspects of the traumatic event

Keeping busy

Losing interest in certain activities that were once enjoyable and even in life in general

Feeling emotionally numb, cut-off and disconnected from others

Avoiding places, objects, events, situations, and even thoughts and feelings that could serve as reminders of the trauma

Increased alertness, anxiety, and emotional arousal

A person suffering from PTSD is also known to experience constant symptoms of increased alertness, anxiety and emotional arousal and may tend to show the following:

Constant feeling of being on edge or tensed

Being very easily startled

Having difficulty concentrating

Panicking when reminded of the traumatic event

Having difficulty sleeping

Being easily upset and irritable

Having angry or violent outbursts

Hyper-vigilance or extreme alertness

Aggressive, dangerous, and even self-destructive behavior

The various symptoms of Post-Traumatic Stress Disorder particularly make it very difficult to live a normal and productive life or to build and maintain healthy and fruitful relationships after the trauma. Taking care of important tasks also become exceptionally difficult and could in turn, lead to the overall decline of the person's quality of life.

If not treated right away, PTSD may lead to other more serious complications including:

Alcohol and drug abuse

Depression

Phobias

Eating disorders

Suicidal tendencies

Chapter 8: How to deal with the trauma

It's normal to be apprehensive in the wake of something frightening or hazardous occurs. At the point when you feel you're in risk, your body reacts with a surge of synthetic compounds that make you increasingly alert. This is known as the "flight or battle" reaction. It causes us endure perilous occasions.

Be that as it may, the cerebrum's reaction to terrifying occasions can likewise prompt constant issues. This can incorporate issue dozing; feeling nervous habitually; being effectively alarmed, on edge, or jittery; having flashbacks; or maintaining a strategic distance from things that help you to remember the occasion.

In some cases these side effects leave following half a month. However, now and again they last any longer. On the off chance that indications last over a month and become serious enough to meddle with connections or work, it might be an indication of post-awful pressure issue, or PTSD.

"There are genuine neurobiological results of injury that are related with PTSD," clarifies Dr. Farris Tuma, who directs the NIH awful pressure research program. NIH-supported scientists are revealing the science behind these mind changes and searching for approaches to counteract and treat PTSD.

What is Trauma?

"A great many people partner post-awful pressure side effects with veterans and battle circumstances," says Dr. Amit Etkin, a NIH-subsidized emotional wellness master at Stanford University. "Notwithstanding, a wide range of injury occur during one's life that can prompt post-horrible pressure issue and post-awful pressure issue like manifestations."

This incorporates individuals who have experienced a physical or rape, misuse, a mishap, a catastrophe, or numerous different genuine occasions.

Anybody can create PTSD, at any age. As per the National Center for Post-Traumatic Stress Disorder, around 7 or 8 out of each 100 individuals will encounter PTSD sooner or later in their lives.

"We don't have a blood test that would let you know or inquiry you can pose to someone to know whether they're in the most elevated hazard bunch for creating PTSD," Tuma says. "However, we do realize that there are a few things that expansion chance by and large and a few things that secure against it."

Science of Traumatic Stress

Analysts are investigating what puts individuals in danger for PTSD. One group, drove by Dr. Samuel McLean, an injury master at the University of North Carolina, is examining how post-horrible pressure side effects create in the cerebrum. They will pursue 5,000 injury survivors for one year.

"We're enlisting individuals who visit injury focuses following an injury since proof proposes that a great deal of the significant natural changes that lead to steady side effects occur in the early fallout of the injury," McLean says.

They're gathering data about existence history preceding injury, distinguishing post-awful side effects, gathering hereditary and different kinds of organic information, and performing mind filters. The examination is additionally utilizing keen watches and PDA applications to gauge the body's reaction to injury. These devices will assist scientists with revealing how injury influences individuals' day by day lives, for example, their action, rest, and state of mind.

"Our objective is that there will be when injury survivors come in for consideration and get screening and mediations to avert

PTSD, just similarly that they would be screened with X-beams to set broken bones," McLean clarifies.

Adapting To Trauma

How you respond when something awful occurs, and in the blink of an eye a short time later, can help or defer your recuperation.

"It's imperative to have an adapting methodology for overcoming the awful sentiments of a horrible mishap," Tuma says. A decent adapting methodology, he clarifies, is discovering someone to converse with about your emotions. A terrible adapting system would turn liquor or medications.

Having a positive adapting procedure and taking in something from the circumstance can assist you with recuperating from a horrible accident. So can looking for help from companions, family, or a care group.

Chatting with an emotional well-being proficient can assist somebody with post-horrendous pressure side effects figure out how to adapt. It's significant for anybody with PTSD-like side effects to be treated by a psychological well-being proficient who is prepared in injury centered treatment.

A self improvement site and applications created by the U.S. Branch of Veterans Affairs can likewise offer help when you need it following an injury.

"For the individuals who start treatment and experience it, an enormous level of those will show signs of improvement and will get some help," Tuma says. A few drugs can help treat certain indications, as well.

PTSD influences individuals in an unexpected way, so a treatment that works for one individual may not work for another. A few people with PTSD need to attempt various medications to discover what works for their manifestations.

Discovering Treatments

"While we right now analyze this as one issue in psychiatry, in truth, there's a great deal of variety among individuals and the sorts of side effects that they have," Etkin says.

These distinctions can make it hard to discover a treatment that works. Etkin's group is attempting to comprehend why a few people's minds react to treatment and others don't.

"PTSD is extremely normal. In any case, the assortment of ways that it shows in the mind is huge," Etkin clarifies. "We don't have the foggiest idea what number of fundamental conditions there are, or particular mind issues there are, that lead to PTSD. So we're attempting to make sense of that part."

His group has recognized cerebrum circuits that show when treatment is working. They've discovered a different cerebrum circuit that can anticipate who will react to treatment.

His gathering is presently trying a procedure called noninvasive cerebrum incitement for individuals who don't react to treatment. They trust that animating certain mind circuits will make treatment progressively compelling.

A great many people recoup normally from injury. Be that as it may, it can require significant investment. In case you're having indications for a really long time—or that are excessively extreme—chat with your medicinal services supplier or a psychological wellness proficient. In the midst of emergency, call the National Suicide Prevention Lifeline at 1-800-273-TALK (8255) or visit the crisis room.

"PTSD is genuine. This isn't a shortcoming in any capacity," Tuma clarifies.

"Individuals shouldn't battle alone and peacefully."

Chapter 9: Boost your serotonin levels to ward off insomnia and depression

We experience different kinds of depressions of our central nervous systems if we are low on certain hormones. Did you know that you can effectively change your hormones through your food, drinks and exercise regimen?

As we said earlier, exercise boosts your serotonin levels as much as Prozac, an anti-depressant medication. Many people still feel depressed after taking anti-depressants because most anti-depressant medications only elevate one hormone and not the other. Both hormones must be in balance with one another in order for you to feel good. This is where your diet comes in.

Signs of low serotonin include intrusive nighttime thoughts, waking up in the middle of the night, having trouble falling asleep, etc. Low serotonin hormone can cause negative thinking, and it can cause you to become pessimistic and distrustful. You might feel as though you are anxious, nervous, and ready to have a panic attack at any moment. You will suffer from insomnia most nights. Little things set you off; you are agitated and worrisome. Do you have suicidal thoughts occasionally, or are you aggressive or violent at times? Do you struggle to control your temper? Do you pick at others or become critical, fussy or judgmental toward others at times, when you aren't normally like that?

Women and men experience serotonin deficiency differently. Women experience low serotonin levels as depression, anxiety, and insomnia symptoms whereas men experience low serotonin as problems with impulsivity, attention deficits, lack of self-control, and a tendency to self-medicate to make oneself feel better.

Low serotonin in women can manifest also in muscle pain (like fibromyalgia), TMJ (grinding your teeth and biting and jaw pain), tension headaches or migraines, diarrhea or constipation issues, stomach aches, weight issues, overeating, food cravings, eating disorders, and breathing difficulties.

When your serotonin levels (and other hormone levels in your body) are at their optimal levels, you will feel happy, positive, confident, and flexible. You will have a more agreeable and positive and generous attitude, and other people will react very differently to you, too. Other people can tell when your hormone levels are off because you don't smile or have confident body language. People will be more helpful to you when you look more confident and happier on the outside, even if you feel weak on the inside. Predators like Ted Bundy have bragged that they specifically prey on people who lack confidence when they walk, for example.

Another sign of low serotonin is craving sweets and starches. These foods generally boost your hormones on a temporary basis, which is why you crave them. However, eating them consistently will make you sedentary and overweight. You should be trying to get your serotonin boost from exercising. The next time you are craving sweets and starches, head to the gym or take a walk, or eat the foods that are on the healthy list below.

Foods that boost your serotonin in healthy ways include: asparagus, avocado, salmon, fish and fish oils, omega 3s, dark chocolate (not milk chocolate), spinach, walnuts, oats, coffee (use sparingly), pineapple, eggplant, pecans, bananas, brown rice, turkey, whole grain breads, whole grain pastas, potatoes, parsnips, peas, lentils, nuts, seeds, and seed oils, including flax seed.

Sun also helps boost your serotonin levels, so make sure you get outside.

Chapter 10: Exercise as a Treatment for PTSD

Doctors are increasingly prescribing exercise as medicine for their patients to prevent and treat disease and injury. A growing collection of evidence also suggests that exercise can be therapeutic for individuals suffering from Posttraumatic Stress Disorder, including victims of rape. Research being presented today at the 58th Annual Meeting of the American College of Sports Medicine and 2nd World Congress on Exercise is Medicine® evaluated the effect of exercise for anxiety disorder that affects up to 15 percent of the general population, including approximately 50 percent of female rape victims.

"Preliminary research has revealed that aerobic exercise may be an effective treatment for PTSD," said Erika Smith, lead author of this study. "Previous studies have not utilized a control group and have not compared aerobic exercise to an empirically validated treatment for PTSD. This study aimed to do just that."

Smith and her colleagues from the University of West Florida studied 14 participants who were recruited naturalistically through a Certified Rape Crisis Center in Pensacola, Fla. All participants attended bi-weekly cognitive behavioral therapy sessions, and seven of the participants also attended a minimum of two group circuit training classes per week.

The therapy sessions consisted of cognitive behavior interventions (CBT) as outlined by Dr. Edna Foa. Exercise sessions were 40 minutes in duration, including full-body exercises, and the circuit consisted of 30 seconds per exercise. The research team recorded each participant's PTSD symptoms before and after treatment using the PTSD Checklist - Specific Versions (PCL-S).

Participants from both groups experienced improvement. Based on the study, Smith and her colleagues call for more research on the benefits of aerobic exercise as an adjunct treatment for individuals diagnosed with PTSD and a history of having experienced trauma.

The National Institute of Mental Health (NIMH)

The following is what (NIMH) has this to say about PTSD:

When in danger, it's natural to feel fear. This fear may trigger many split-second changes in the body to prepare to defend against the danger or to avoid it. This "fight-or-flight" response is a **healthy reaction** meant to protect a person from harm. **But in post-traumatic stress disorder, this reaction is changed or damaged. People who have PTSD may**

feel stressed or frightened even when they're no longer in danger.

PTSD develops after a terrifying ordeal that involved physical harm or the threat of physical harm. The person who develops PTSD may have been the one who was harmed or the harm may have happened to a loved one or the person may have witnessed a harmful event that happened to loved ones, comrades or strangers.

PTSD was first brought to public attention in relation to war veterans, but it can result from a variety of traumatic incidents, such as mugging, rape, torture, being kidnapped or held captive, child abuse, car accidents, train wrecks, plane crashes, bombings, or natural disasters such as floods or earthquakes.

Causes

Currently, many scientists are focusing on genes that play a role in creating fear memories. Understanding how fear memories are created may help to refine or find new interventions for reducing the symptoms of PTSD. For example, PTSD researchers have pinpointed genes that make:

Stathmin, a protein needed to form fear memories. In one study, mice that did not make stathmin were less likely than normal mice to "freeze," a natural, protective response to danger, after being exposed to a fearful experience. They also showed less innate fear by exploring open spaces more willingly than normal mice.

GRP (gastrin-releasing peptide), a signaling chemical in the brain released during emotional events. In mice, GRP seems to help control the fear response, and lack of GRP may lead to the creation of greater and more lasting memories of fear.

Researchers have also found a version of the 5-HTTLPR gene, which controls levels of serotonin — a brain chemical related to mood-that appears to fuel the fear response. Like other mental disorders, it is likely that many genes with small effects are at work in PTSD.

Brain Areas. Studying parts of the brain involved in dealing with fear and stress also helps researchers to better understand possible causes of PTSD. One such brain structure is the amygdala, known for its role in emotion, learning, and memory. The **amygdala** appears to be active in fear acquisition, or learning to fear an event (such as touching a hot stove), as well as in the early stages of fear extinction, or learning not to fear.

Storing extinction memories and dampening the original fear response appears to involve the **prefrontal cortex** (PFC), which is involved in tasks such as decision-making, problem-solving, and judgment. Certain areas of the PFC play slightly different roles. For example, when it deems a source of stress controllable, the medial PFC suppresses the amygdala, an alarm center deep in the brainstem and controls the stress response. The ventromedial PFC helps sustain long-term extinction of fearful memories, and **the size of this brain area may affect its ability to do so.**

Individual differences in these genes or brain areas may only set the stage for PTSD without actually causing symptoms. Environmental factors, such as childhood trauma, head injury, or a history of mental illness, may further increase a person's risk by affecting the early growth of the brain. Also, personality and cognitive factors, such as optimism and the tendency to view challenges in a positive or negative way, as well as social factors, such as the availability and use of social support, appear to influence how people adjust to trauma. More research may show what combinations of these or perhaps other factors could be used someday to predict who will develop PTSD following a traumatic event.

The Future for PTSD Research

In the last decade, rapid progress in research on the mental and biological foundations of PTSD has lead scientists to focus on prevention as a realistic and important goal.

For example, NIMH-funded researchers are exploring new and orphan medications (unassociated with any regimen) thought to target underlying causes of PTSD in an effort to prevent the disorder. Other research is attempting to enhance cognitive, personality, and social protective factors and to minimize risk factors to ward off full-blown PTSD after trauma. Still other research is attempting to identify what factors determine whether someone with PTSD will respond well to one type of intervention or another, aiming to develop more personalized, effective and efficient treatments.

As gene research and brain imaging technologies continue to improve, scientists are more likely to be able to pinpoint when and where in the brain PTSD begins. This understanding may then lead to better targeted treatments to suit each person's own needs or even prevent the disorder before it causes harm.

Signs & Symptoms

PTSD can cause many symptoms. These symptoms can be grouped into three categories:

1. Re-experiencing Symptoms

Flashbacks—reliving the trauma over and over, including physical symptoms like a racing heart or sweating

Bad dreams

Frightening thoughts.

Re-experiencing symptoms may cause problems in a person's everyday routine. They can start from the person's own thoughts and feelings. Words, objects, or situations that are reminders of the event can also trigger re-experiencing.

2. Avoidance Symptoms

Staying away from places, events, or objects that are reminders of the experience

Feeling emotionally numb

Feeling strong guilt, depression, or worry

Losing interest in activities that were enjoyable in the past

Having trouble remembering the dangerous event.

Things that remind a person of the traumatic event can trigger avoidance symptoms. These symptoms may cause a person to change his or her personal routine. For example, after a bad car accident, a person who usually drives may avoid driving or riding in a car.

3. Hyperarousal Symptoms

Being easily startled

Feeling tense or "on edge"

Having difficulty sleeping, and/or having angry outbursts.

Hyperarousal symptoms are usually constant, instead of being triggered by things that remind one of the traumatic event. They can make the person feel stressed and angry. These symptoms may make it hard to do daily tasks, such as sleeping, eating, or concentrating.

It's natural to have some of these symptoms after a dangerous event. Sometimes people have very serious symptoms that go away after a few weeks. This is called acute stress disorder, or ASD. When the symptoms last more than a few weeks and become an ongoing problem, they might be PTSD. Some people with PTSD don't show any symptoms for weeks or months.

Do Children React Differently Than Adults?

Children and teens can have extreme reactions to trauma, but their symptoms may not be the same as adults. In very young children, these symptoms can include:

Bedwetting, when they'd learned how to use the toilet before

Forgetting how or being unable to talk

Acting out the scary event during playtime

Being unusually clingy with a parent or other adult.

Older children and teens usually show symptoms more like those seen in adults. They may also develop disruptive, disrespectful, or destructive behaviors. Older children and teens may feel guilty for not preventing injury or deaths. They may also have thoughts of revenge. For more information, see the NIMH booklets on helping children cope with violence and disasters.

Who Is At Risk?

PTSD affects about 7.7 million American adults, but it can occur at any age, including childhood. Women are more likely to develop PTSD than men, and there is some evidence that susceptibility to the disorder may run in families.

Anyone can get PTSD at any age. This includes war veterans and survivors of physical and sexual assault, abuse, accidents, disasters, and many other serious events.

Not everyone with PTSD has been through a dangerous event. Some people get PTSD after a friend or family member experiences danger or is harmed. The sudden, unexpected death of a loved one can also cause PTSD.

Why Do Some Get PTSD And Others People Do Not?

It is important to remember that not everyone who lives through a dangerous event gets PTSD. In fact, most will not get the disorder.

Many factors play a part in whether a person will get PTSD. Some of these are risk factors that make a person more likely to get PTSD. Other factors, called resilience factors, can help reduce the risk of the disorder. Some of these risk and resilience factors are present before the trauma and others become important during and after a traumatic event.

Risk Factors For PTSD Include:

Living through dangerous events and traumas

Having a history of mental illness

Mental, emotional, and physical hurt

Witnessing people hurt or killed

Feeling horror, helplessness, or extreme fear

Having little or no social support after a traumatic event

Dealing with extra stress after the event, such as loss of a loved one, pain and injury, or loss of a job or home.

Resilience factors that may reduce the risk of PTSD include:

Seeking out support from other people, such as friends and family

Finding a support group after a traumatic event

Feeling good about one's own actions in the face of danger

Having a coping strategy, or a way of getting through the bad event and learning from it

Being able to act and respond effectively despite feeling fear.

Researchers are studying the importance of various risk and resilience factors. With more study, it may be possible someday to predict who is likely to get PTSD and prevent it.

Diagnosis

Not every traumatized person develops full-blown or even minor PTSD. **Symptoms usually begin within 3 months of the incident but occasionally emerge years afterward. They must last more than a month to be considered PTSD.** The course of the illness varies. Some people recover within 6 months, while others have symptoms that last much longer. In some people, the condition becomes chronic.

A doctor who has experience helping people with mental illnesses, such as a psychiatrist or psychologist, can diagnose PTSD. The diagnosis is made after the doctor talks with the person who has symptoms of PTSD.

To be diagnosed with PTSD, a person must have all of the following for at least 1 month:

At least one re-experiencing symptom

At least three avoidance symptoms

At least two hyperarousal symptoms

Symptoms that make it hard to go about daily life, go to school or work, be with friends, and take care of important tasks.

PTSD is often accompanied by depression, substance abuse, or one or more of the other anxiety disorders.

Treatments

The main treatments for people with PTSD are psychotherapy ("talk" therapy), medications, or both. Everyone is different, so a treatment that works for one person may not work for another. It is important for anyone with PTSD to be treated by a mental health care provider who is experienced with PTSD. **Some people with PTSD need to try different treatments to find what works for their symptoms.**

If someone with PTSD is going through an ongoing trauma, such as being in an abusive relationship, both of the problems need to be treated. Other ongoing problems can include panic disorder, depression, substance abuse, and feeling suicidal.

Psychotherapy

Psychotherapy is "talk" therapy. It involves talking with a mental health professional to treat a mental illness. Psychotherapy can occur one-on-one or in a group. Talk therapy treatment for PTSD usually lasts 6 to 12 weeks, but can take more time. Research shows that support from family and friends can be an important part of therapy.

Many types of psychotherapy can help people with PTSD. Some types target the symptoms of PTSD directly. Other therapies focus on social, family, or job-related problems. The doctor or therapist may combine different therapies depending on each person's needs.

One helpful therapy is called cognitive behavioral therapy, or CBT. There are several parts to CBT, including:

Exposure therapy. This therapy helps people face and control their fear. It exposes them to the trauma they experienced in a safe way. It uses mental imagery, writing, or visits to the place where the event happened. The therapist uses these tools to help people with PTSD cope with their feelings.

Cognitive restructuring. This therapy helps people make sense of the bad memories. Sometimes people remember the event differently than how it happened. They may feel guilt or shame about what is not their fault. The therapist helps people with PTSD look at what happened in a realistic way.

Stress inoculation training. This therapy tries to reduce PTSD symptoms by teaching a person how to reduce anxiety. Like cognitive restructuring, this treatment helps people look at their memories in a healthy way.

Other types of treatment can also help people with PTSD. People with PTSD should talk about all treatment options with their therapist.

How Talk Therapies Help People Overcome PTSD

Talk therapies teach people helpful ways to react to frightening events that trigger their PTSD symptoms. Based on this general goal, different types of therapy may:

Teach about trauma and its effects.

Use relaxation and anger control skills.

Provide tips for better sleep, diet, and exercise habits.

Help people identify and deal with guilt, shame, and other feelings about the event.

Focus on changing how people react to their PTSD symptoms. For example, therapy helps people visit places and people that are reminders of the trauma.

Medications

The U.S. Food and Drug Administration (FDA) has approved two medications for treating adults with PTSD:

sertraline (Zoloft)

paroxetine (Paxil)

Both of these medications are antidepressants, which are also used to treat depression. They may help control PTSD symptoms such as sadness, worry, anger, and feeling numb inside. Taking these medications may make it easier to go through psychotherapy.

Since medications affect everyone differently, any side effects or unusual reactions should be reported to a doctor immediately.

The most common side effects of antidepressants like sertraline and paroxetine are:

Headache, which usually goes away within a few days.

Nausea (feeling sick to your stomach), which usually goes away within a few days.

Sleeplessness or drowsiness, which may occur during the first few weeks but then goes away.

Agitation (feeling jittery).

Sexual problems, which can affect both men and women, including reduced sex drive, and problems having and enjoying sex.

Sometimes the medication dose needs to be reduced or the time of day it is taken needs to be adjusted to help lessen these side effects.

FDA Warning on Antidepressants

Despite the relative safety and popularity of antidepressants, some studies have suggested that they may have unintentional effects on some people, especially adolescents and young adults. In 2004, the U.S. Food and Drug Administration (FDA) conducted a thorough review of published and unpublished controlled clinical trials of antidepressants that involved nearly 4,400 children and adolescents. The review revealed that 4 percent of those taking antidepressants thought about or attempted suicide (although no suicides occurred), compared to 2 percent of those receiving placebos.

This information prompted the FDA in 2005, to adopt a "black box" warning label on all antidepressant medications to alert the public about the potential increased risk of suicidal thinking or attempts in children and adolescents taking antidepressants. In 2007, the FDA proposed that makers of all antidepressant medications extend the warning to include young adults up through age 24. **A "black box" warning is the most serious type of warning on prescription drug labeling**.

The warning emphasizes that patients of all ages taking antidepressants should be closely monitored, especially during the initial weeks of treatment. Possible side effects to look for are worsening depression, suicidal thinking or behavior, or any unusual changes in behavior such as sleeplessness, agitation, or withdrawal from normal social situations. The warning adds that families and caregivers should also be told of the need for close monitoring and report any changes to the physician. The latest information can be found on the FDA website.

Results of a comprehensive review of pediatric trials conducted between 1988 and 2006 suggested that the benefits of antidepressant medications likely outweigh their risks to children and adolescents with major depression and anxiety disorders. The study was funded in part by the National Institute of Mental Health (NIMH).

Other Medications

Doctors may also prescribe other types of medications, such as the ones listed below. There is little information on how well these work for people with PTSD.

1.**Benzodiazepines.** These medications may be given to help people relax and sleep. People who take benzodiazepines may have memory problems or become dependent on the medication.

2.**Antipsychotics.** These medications are usually given to people with other mental disorders, like schizophrenia. People who take antipsychotics may gain weight and have a higher chance of getting heart disease and diabetes.

3.**Other antidepressants.** Like sertraline and paroxetine, the antidepressants fluoxetine (Prozac) and citalopram (Celexa) can help people with PTSD feel less tense or sad. For people with PTSD who also have other anxiety disorders or depression, antidepressants may be useful in reducing symptoms of these co-occurring illnesses.

Treatment After Mass Trauma

Sometimes large numbers of people are affected by the same event. For example, a lot of people needed help after Hurricane Katrina in 2005 and the terrorist attacks of September 11, 2001. Most people will have some PTSD symptoms in the first few weeks after events like these. This is a normal and expected response to serious trauma, and for most people, symptoms generally lessen with time. Most people can be helped with basic support, such as:

Getting to a safe place

Seeing a doctor if injured

Getting food and water

Contacting loved ones or friends

Learning what is being done to help.

But some people do not get better on their own. A study of Hurricane Katrina survivors found that, over time, more people were having problems with PTSD, depression, and related mental disorders. This pattern is unlike the recovery from other natural disasters, where the number of people who have mental health problems gradually lessens. As communities try to rebuild after a mass trauma, people may experience ongoing stress from loss of jobs and schools, and trouble paying bills, finding housing, and getting health care. This delay in community recovery may in turn delay recovery from PTSD.

In the first couple weeks after a mass trauma, brief versions of Cognitive Behavioral Therapy (CBT) may be helpful to some people who are having severe distress. Sometimes other treatments are used, but their effectiveness is not known. For example, there is growing interest in an approach called psychological first aid. The goal of this approach is to make people feel safe and secure, connect people to health care and other resources, and reduce stress reactions. There are guides for carrying out the treatment, but experts do not know yet if it helps prevent or treat PTSD.

In single-session psychological debriefing, another type of mass trauma treatment, survivors talk about the event and express their feelings one-on-one or in a group. Studies show that it is not likely to reduce distress or the risk for PTSD, and may actually increase distress and risk.

Mass Trauma Affects Hospitals and Other Providers

Hospitals, health care systems, and health care providers are also affected by a mass trauma. The number of people who need immediate physical and psychological help may be too much for health systems to handle. Some patients may not find help when they need it because hospitals do not have enough staff or supplies. In some cases, health care providers themselves may be struggling to recover as well.

NIMH scientists are working on this problem. For example, researchers are testing how to give CBT and other treatments using the phone and the Internet. In one study, people with PTSD met with a therapist to learn about the disorder, made a list of things that trigger their symptoms, and learned basic ways to reduce stress. After this meeting, the participants could visit a website with more information about PTSD. Participants could keep a log of their symptoms and practice coping skills. Overall, the researchers found the Internet-based treatment helped reduce symptoms of PTSD and depression. These effects lasted after treatment ended.

Researchers will carry out more studies to find out if other such approaches to therapy can be helpful after mass trauma.

Size of the Problem

Given the size of the problem with PTSD, the VA and the NIMH will continue research into the best cure, not just "First-aid" for this malady. Given our propensity for war we need fixes, not band-aids for this serious condition!

Chapter 11: Managing Stress - The Basics

Though stress can wreak havoc on your life, a stress management strategy can seem overwhelming in its own right. Almost always, when I first recommend stress management to people, their first response is that they don't have time, they're too busy, it's too much work, or, most commonly of all, that they've already tried stress management and it didn't work.

But none of these things are true. At least, not if you don't want them to be. If you feel like you don't have the time or you're too busy to manage your stress, don't worry. It's okay to go slow, and go at a pace that works best for you. There are no deadlines in stress management. If you only have 10 minutes a day to spare, that's fine. If you only have 10 minutes a week to spare, that's fine too. The only important thing is to stay committed and put yourself on a regular schedule. Don't tell yourself you'll do it "whenever you have time." If you do that, you'll never get around to it, and give up before you've really even started.

Stress management is a skill, and like all skills, it takes time and practice to learn. You can't master it overnight, no matter how hard you try. So you might as well go slow. Overwhelming yourself will actually increase your stress - the opposite of what stress management is supposed to do. For ideal results, 15 minutes a day is the recommended time to devote to a daily stress management technique (Avoiding Roadblocks to Stress Reduction, 2016). This might sound like a long time, but that 15 minutes can happen during a coffee break, a lunch hour, the moment that you get home from work, or during your morning commute.

If you are resistant to taking on a new project or feel like stress management is simply too much work, just remember that there is no one right way to manage your stress. Everyone's stressors are unique, and everyone's idea of relaxation is different. A beach in the Caribbean might sound like heaven to you, but it might sound like hell to someone else. Don't be afraid to drop or modify a stress management technique if it doesn't work for you. But remember, it may take awhile before many of these techniques start to show results. If you begin to dread your designated 15 minutes of daily meditation, try instead to experiment with different kinds of meditation, or even move on to a different technique entirely.

That being said, try to keep your mind open and give new things a try. Some of these stress reduction techniques might feel a little strange or uncomfortable at first. Some may be familiar to you, while others might be completely new. With increasing amounts of stress in the world, different stress management techniques may have gained mainstream attention.

This is both a good and a bad thing. For example, you may have heard of breathing exercises before, or even tried a few of them yourself. But the context in which you were introduced to this concept can sometimes affect the way that you think about it. Try to have an open mind, and give these techniques an honest try before you rule them out. You might be surprised at what starts to work for you once you find a way to work it comfortably into your daily routine.

Most methods and techniques require practice before you get them completely right. Approach stress management the same way you would approach learning to ride a bike or drive a car. You won't do it perfectly the first time. Or the second. Or even the third. Though stress management can seem like an intellectual pursuit, it's not enough to only read about it. Anyone can understand how to drive a car from a simple explanation. But to get behind the wheel is a different kind of learning. When you try out a stress management technique, you get behind the wheel, so to speak. So be patient, be open, and eventually you will get into a style and rhythm that is comfortable for you.

It is very important to practice stress management techniques in a quiet place. Don't wait until you're in a stressful situation to apply these tactics. Think about it like learning an instrument. You need to practice every single day, so that when the day of the concert arrives, you already know what to do. Stress management keeps your stress levels low all the time, so that when you are faced with a stressful situation, you're able to keep calm and confident. However, a quiet place can be difficult to find if you lead a hectic and busy life, so you might have to settle for places that are less glamorous. If you have your own office, that's a great place to practice undisturbed. If you have your own bedroom, that's another good option. Wherever you choose, try to find a space that's relatively private, where you won't be disturbed by others.

Don't feel the need to embark on this journey alone! If someone else in your life is also dealing with stress and anxiety, ask if they want to practice with you. Many self-care routines, like weight loss or going to the gym, are far more effective when you have someone else to do it with. Stress management is the same. You won't feel as alone or self-conscious if you have someone else to practice with, and you're far more likely to stay committed if you have a friend to cheer you on.

Above all, don't expect overnight results. The stress you're experiencing took years and years to build, and so it may take just as long to completely overcome. That's not meant to scare or discourage you, however. Stress management doesn't have to be an invasive or difficult process, but no matter what, it will be a slow one. Don't get impatient with yourself, and don't be too quick to give up on something that isn't yielding the results you want. Go slow, go easy, and don't be too hard on yourself.

How to Measure Your Stress

How can you measure a feeling? Fortunately for doctors and psychologists, stress isn't just something you **feel**. It also affects your behaviors and your physical wellness. For doctors, stress levels can be easily tracked by looking at physical markers, including blood, urine, and even saliva tests that measure the levels of stress hormones present in your body (Figueroa-Fankhanel, 2014). But stress can also be measured from a psychological perspective. Some methods, like observation and interviews, are conducted by professionals. But there are a number of easy strategies you can employ to measure your stress levels on your own. The following 3-Step Process is a very simple one that will help you check in on your own stress levels. It will help you be more aware of how stress affects you, and help you keep track of your progress as you begin employing techniques for stress management.

Do a Gut Check

It may seem obvious, but the first step in measuring your stress level is to simply take a step back and ask yourself, "How do I feel?" A gut check is simply giving yourself a second to check in with your body and mind and determine how you're feeling. Remember that stress presents in everyone's body in slightly different ways. If you find yourself feeling stress, take a moment to observe the situation. How would you rate your stress, on a scale from one to ten (one being very low, ten being extremely high)? Think about your physical symptoms. What's happening in your body? Do you feel pain or tension anywhere? Are you experiencing digestive troubles? Are you having trouble performing sexually? Understanding where and how stress is stored in your body will help you to understand just how stressed you are in any given situation. Sometimes we become so used to dealing with stress that we don't even realize how severe our stress is until our body presents with physical symptoms.

Next, observe your mood. Are you feeling depressed? Anxious? Angry? Just as different people's bodies express stress differently, your mind expresses stress in unique ways too. Learning how you emotionally respond to stress is just as important as learning what your physical symptoms are. Some people become extremely depressed when they're under a lot of stress. Other people feel extremely nervous or anxious. The ways that you emotionally respond to stress will give you clues as to what steps are best for you when it comes to managing your stress successfully.

Use a Stress Gauge

The most commonly used psychological tool to measure stress levels is called the Perceived Stress Scale, or PSS. If you're someone who likes specificity and you want a more concrete way to measure your stress, there are a number of PSS tests and tools available for free online from reliable websites. This test will give you a number between 0-40 to determine how severe your stress levels are. The test asks you to think about your life over the course of the past month, and so it's most useful when conducted on a monthly basis.

Make Yourself a Stress Journal

This can be a physical notebook, a document in your computer, or a dedicated desk drawer. Whatever form it takes, your stress journal is going to be your most important tool as you move forward with your stress management journey. Keeping a record of your stress levels will help you to determine if your stress management techniques are working, and will give you valuable information about yourself that you will need to make the necessary adjustments. Keeping notes in your stress journal does not have to be a difficult task. All you need is 5 minutes a day to update your journal and check in with your emotional and physical wellbeing.

Conclusion

Post-traumatic stress disorder (PTSD) may affect many different people. This is a very common disorder, and many people tend to have this more than we may know these days. Each sign and symptom of PTSD may also be different from person to person. The signs and symptoms that may be present in someone who has this disorder may be reliving a horrible event through flashbacks, dreams or even nightmares. PTSD does not have a specific age limit but most men do seem to experience this disorder more than most women do. Psychological effects are very common within someone who has experienced PTSD. They are often reliving their traumatic experience within their memory. Treatments that have been proven to work for PSTD have been medication and psychotherapy. After reading all the efficient techniques and therapies to cope with stress and PTSD, a person has find the right type of medication and treatment that can work right for them.